CAMBRIDGE HITACHI

PENPALS for Handwriting

Pack of 10

Year 2 / Primary 3 Workbook

University Printing House, Cambridge CB2 8BS, United Kingdom
One Liberty Plaza, 20th Floor, New York, NY 10006, USA
477 Williamstown Road, Port Melbourne, VIC 3207, Australia
4843/24, 2nd Floor, Ansari Road, Daryaganj, Delhi – 110002, India
79 Anson Road, #06–04/06, Singapore 079906

Cambridge University Press is part of the University of Cambridge.

It furthers the University's mission by disseminating knowledge in the pursuit of education, learning and research at the highest international levels of excellence.

Information on this title: education.cambridge.org

© Cambridge-Hitachi 2015
First published 2015
20 19 18 17 16 15 14

Printed in Poland by Opolgraf

A catalogue record for this publication is available from the British Library

ISBN 978-1-84565-298-2

Acknowledgements
Illustrations by Marek Jagucki
Cover design and layout by me&him
Authors: Gill Budgell and Kate Ruttle

www.cambridge.org

ISBN 978-1-84565-298-2

Penpals *for* Handwriting

Workbook

2

Name _____ Class _____

Unit 1

Practising diagonal join to ascender

1 Trace and write the joins.

ch _____ _____   *th* _____ _____

2 Trace and write the words.

choose   chews   their   there

_____   _____   _____   _____

3 Trace the writing. Write one of the words above in each gap.

They _____

_____ in the sweet shop.

4 Write a sentence for each word: *there*, *their* **and** *they're*

_____

_____

_____

Check:
- you have joined *th* and *ch*
- you have used the correct word.

Find one word to tick and one to improve.

2

Practising diagonal join, no ascender S Unit 2

1 Trace and write the joins.

ai _____ _____   ay _____ _____

2 Trace and write the words.

snail   train   today

_____ _____ _____

3 Choose *ai* or *ay* to finish the words. Write the words.

pl___ground   r___ny d___   cr___on

_____ _____ _____

4 Write all the days of the week.

_____   _____   _____

_____   _____

_____

Check:
- you have joined *ai* and *ay*
- you have spelled the word correctly.

Find one word to tick and one to improve.

Unit 3 G

Practising diagonal join, no ascender

1 Trace and write the joins.

ir ___ ___   *er* ___ ___

2 Trace and write the words.

dirtier   *cleaner*   *nicer*

_____   _____   _____

3 Which words can you add *er* to? Write them in the box.

shirt   *short*

small   *firm*

expert   *skirt*

4 Write three more adjectives with an *er* ending.

_____   _____

_____

Check:
- you have written the joins correctly
- the words in the box are all adjectives.

Find one word to tick and one to improve.

Practising horizontal join to ascender

Unit 4

1 Trace and write the joins.

wh _____ _____ oh _____ _____

2 Trace and write the words.

when   which   what   where

_____   _____   _____   _____

3 Trace and write the sentences. Add punctuation.

Is this what I have to do_

_____

That is why we walk in school_

_____

Did you go where I sent you_

_____

4 Put a tick beside the punctuation marks you used.

Check:
- you have joined *wh* correctly
- you have used the correct punctuation.

Find one word to tick and one to improve.

Unit 5

Practising horizontal join, no ascender

1 Trace and write the joins.

ow

ou

ou

ou

2 Trace and write the words.

how

could

would

should

3 Trace the words. Choose a word to start each question. Add punctuation marks.

_____ you like to play
_____ I do it this way
_____ you help me

4 Put a tick beside the punctuation marks you used.

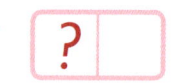  

5 Write another sentence using one of the words.

_____

_____

Check:
- you have joined *ow* and *ou*
- you have written *?* clearly.

Find one word to tick and one to improve.

Introducing diagonal join to *e*

S Unit 6

1 Trace and write the joins.

ie   *ue*

2 Trace and write the words.

baby   babies   jelly   jellies

3 Trace the words. Write the plurals.

lady   cry   blueberry   family

4 Find three more plurals ending in *ies*.

Check:
- you have joined *ie* and *ue*
- the plurals are spelled correctly.

Find one word to tick and one to improve.

Unit 7 G

Introducing horizontal join to *e*

1 Trace and write the joins.

oe ___ ___   ve ___ ___

2 Trace and write the words.

give   live   move

___   ___   ___

3 Trace the verbs. Write the present tense of the verbs.

Present	Past
___	gave
___	moved
___	lived
___	had

4 Write the present and past tenses of the verbs.

Verb	Present	Past
to save	___	___
to dive	___	___

Check:
- you have joined *ve*
- you have written the present tenses correctly.

Find one word to tick and one to improve.

Introducing *ee* S Unit 8

1 Trace and write the joins.

ee ___ ___   *ee* ___ ___

2 Trace and write the words.

agree   *speech*   *steep*   *sweet*

_____   _____   _____   _____

3 Choose a word from above to add to each suffix. Write the word with its suffix.

-ment _____

-less _____

-ness _____

-ly _____

4 How many other suffixes can you add to *agree* **?**

Check:
- you have joined *ee*
- your spelling of the words with suffixes.

Find one word to tick and one to improve.

Unit 9

Practising diagonal join, no ascender

1 Trace and write the joins.

le ___ ___   *le* ___ ___

2 Same sound, different spelling. Try it.

table   *metal*   *fossil*   *camel*

___   ___   ___   ___

3 Decide how to finish each word: *le il el al*

*squirr*___   *app*___   *penc*___

*bott*___   *ped*___   *tab*___

4 Write three more words ending in *le.*

___   ___

___

Check:
- you have joined *le*
- you have chosen the correct word ending.

Find one word to tick and one to improve.

Writing numbers 1–100 — Unit 10

1 Trace and write the numbers.

1 ___   3 ___   5 ___   7 ___   9 ___
12 ___   14 ___   16 ___   18 ___   20 ___

2 Choose an ending for add to each of the words below. Write the word with its suffix.

seven _____

nine _____

four _____

eight _____

3 Write the word beside the number.

14 _____

7 _____

5 _____

20 _____

4 Write numbers to 100, counting in 10s.

Check:
- you have joined *ee, ou*
- the words are spelled correctly
- the height of the numbers is the same as the capital letters.

Find one word to tick and one to improve.

Unit 11 G

Introducing diagonal join to anticlockwise letters

1 Trace and write the joins.

2 Trace and write the words.

ea   head

ea   feather

ea   measure

ea   breath

3 Make noun phrases by adding an adjective to a noun.

a big head

Adjective	deep golden brown sparkly
Noun	breath head treasure bread

4 Write one more noun phrase.

Check:
- you are using all the joins you know
- your noun phrases include adjectives.

Find one word to tick and one to improve.

Practising diagonal join to anticlockwise letters S Unit 12

1 Trace and write the joins.

igh _____ _____   *igh* _____ _____

2 Same sound, different spelling. Try it.

high   *fly*   *pie*   *mice*

_____   _____   _____   _____

3 Decide whether to write the *igh* or *ie* sound in these words.

cr__d   l__t   fl__t   t__   n__t

_____   _____   _____   _____   _____

4 Write a sentence using three of the words.

_____

_____

Check:
- the joins that you know
- your spelling of the *igh* and *ie* words.

Find one word to tick and one to improve.

Unit 13 (P)

Practising diagonal join to anticlockwise letters

1 Trace and write the joins.

dg ___ ___   ng ___ ___

2 Trace and write the words.

badge   edge   swing   danger

_____ _____ _____ _____

3 Read and fill the gaps in each sentence. Choose *dg* or *ng* to complete each word gap. Choose *?* or *!* to punctuate the end of the sentence.

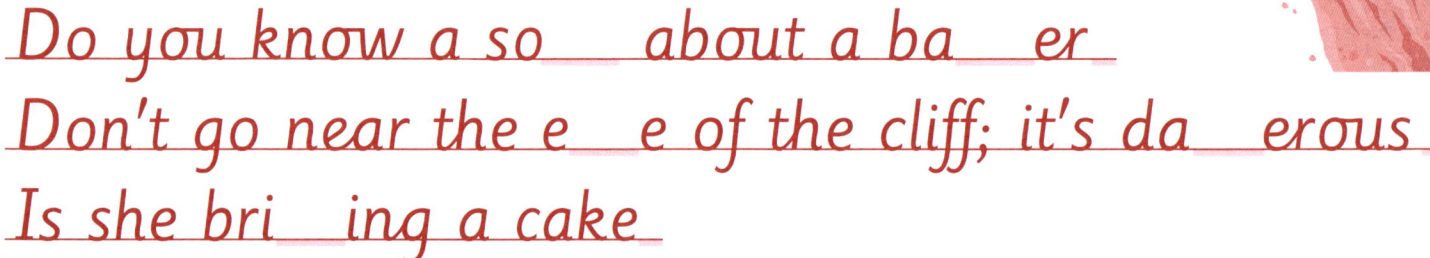

Do you know a so___ about a ba___er

Don't go near the e___e of the cliff; it's da___erous

Is she bri___ing a cake

4 Write a sentence using your own *dg* or *ng* words.

_____

_____

Check:
- you have joined *dg* or *ng* correctly
- the punctuation matches the sentence type.

Find one word to tick and one to improve.

Introducing horizontal join to anticlockwise letters S **Unit 14**

1 Trace and write the joins.

2 Trace and write the words.

3 Trace and write the words. Do the word sums to make compound nouns.

oo

cook

skate + board = _____

foot + ball = _____

oo

room

bed + room = _____

goal + keeper = _____

oa

goal

foot + step = _____

4 Join two short words to make another compound noun.

oa

board

Check:
- joins from o
- spelling of compound nouns.

Find one word to tick and one to improve.

Unit 15

Practising horizontal join to anticlockwise letters

1 Trace and write the joins.

2 Trace and write the words.

3 Trace and write the words. Ring nouns in blue and verbs in red.

wa

want

worm   wok

wa

watch

want   world

wo

two

work   swan

4 Find one word on this page than can be both a noun and a verb. Write it here.

wo

worm

Check:
- you have used all the joins you know
- the nouns are ringed in blue and the verbs in red.

Find one word to tick and one to improve.

Introducing mixed joins for three letters

S Unit 16

1 Trace and write the joins.

air ___ ___   ear ___ ___

2 Trace and write the words.

pair   pear   stair   stare

___ ___ ___ ___

3 Trace the sentence. Choose words from the boxes to fill the gaps.

Is there a ___ hiding under the ___ eating a ___ ?

pair	pear
stair	stare
bear	bare

4 Write a sentence including the words *here* **and** *hear*.

___

___

Check:
- you have used all the joins you know
- you have chosen the correct word each time.

Find one word to tick and one to improve.

17

Unit 17 (s)

Practising mixed joins for three letters

1 Trace and write the joins.

oor _____ _____   our _____ _____

2 Same sound, different spelling. Try it.

poor   pour   flour   flower

_____   _____   _____   _____

3 Trace each sentence. Choose words from the boxes to fill the gaps.

_____ the egg into the _____ slowly.

You can always add a little _____ if you need to.

| poor pour | | moor more | | flour flower |

4 Write a sentence including the words *poor* and *pour*.

_____

_____

Check:
- you have used the joins you know
- you have chosen the right spelling.

Find one word to tick and one to improve.

Practising mixed joins for three letters

G Unit 18

1 Trace and write the joins.

ing _____ *ing* _____

2 Trace and write the words.

shopping   *smiling*   *pouring*

3 Draw the table. Fill in the gaps.

Verb	-ing form	Verb	-ing form
hum	humming	colour	
wait		look	
count		hope	

4 Write a sentence using two -ing words.

_____

_____

Check:
- you have used the joins you know
- the -*ing* words are spelled correctly.

Find one word to tick and one to improve.

Unit 19 G — Size and spacing

1 Trace and write.

so   because   and   when   but

2 Trace and write the sentences. Choose a word to fill the gaps.

She ran fast _____ she was late for school.

He did his homework _____ he did well in the test.

I know what to do _____ I listen in class.

3 Write a sentence with *because*.

Check:
- you have used the joins you know
- your sentences make sense.

Find one word to tick and one to improve.

End-of-term check

Unit 20

1 Write a sentence using each group of words. Add punctuation.

_____

outside we were playing

_____

hard in working class he was

_____

she hand her put up

_____

talking they were quietly

2 Rewrite one of the sentences as a question.

_____

3 Show the punctuation you used.

| ? | | . | |

Check:
- you have used the joins you know
- your sentences make sense and are properly punctuated.

Find one word to tick and one to improve.

Unit 21 G

Building on diagonal join to ascender

1 Trace and write the joins.

ck

al

el

at

ill

2 Trace and write the words.

thick

royal

felt

splat

chilly

3 Read, trace and fill the gap in each noun phrase. Use: *rich*, *royal*, *thick* **and** *chilly*. **Rewrite each noun phrase.**

the _____ palace

_____

some _____ soup

_____

a _____ ice-cream

_____

4 Write a noun phrase using the extra word.

_____

Check:
- you have used the joins you know
- your noun phrases make sense.

Find one word to tick and one to improve.

Building on diagonal join, no ascender

 Unit 22

1 Trace and write the joins.

ui   ey   aw   ur   an   ip

2 Trace and write the words.

monkey   fruit

finger   award

nurse   band

3 Unscramble the noun phrases. Use an apostrophe to show someone or something owns something.

monkeys the fruit	the monkey's fruit
award the nurses	
the engine cars	
dogs paws the	

Check:
- you have used the joins you know
- your noun phrases make sense
- apostrophes are in the right place.

Find one word to tick and one to improve.

Unit 23 P

Building on horizontal join to ascender

1 Trace and write the joins.

2 Trace and write the words.

3 Write a full stop in the correct place. Circle three words that must have a capital letter.

wh

whole

ok

broken

ot

notice

the old globe in the school was broken colin and robin noticed it.

4 Write the passage using the correct punctuation.

ob

obey

ol

old

Check:
- you have used the joins you know
- you have copied the passage correctly with capital letters and full stops.

Find one word to tick and one to improve.

Building on horizontal join, no ascender

G Unit 24

1 Trace and write the joins.

ou

oi

oy

ov

on

op

2 Trace and write the words.

count

join

enjoyed

oven

lesson

opened

3 Read and trace each sentence. Rewrite each sentence in the past tense.

1. She joins the library.
She _____ the library.

2. He loves PE lessons.
_____

3. I enjoy history.
_____

4. I copy the drawings.
_____

Check:
- you have used the joins you know
- your sentences are in the past tense.

Find one word to tick and one to improve.

25

Unit 25 G **Building on diagonal join to anticlockwise letters**

1 Trace and write the joins.

ea ___   ag ___   ed ___   ic ___   eg ___

2 Trace and write the words.

easy _____   flag _____

opened _____   nice _____   leg _____

3 Choose the best option from the box to fill each gap. Write each sentence in full.

Cats are generally _____ than slugs.
_____

| large   largest |
| larger |

Mice are _____ than rats.
_____

| small   smallest |
| smaller |

Adders are not the _____ pets for children.
_____

| good   best |
| better |

Check:
- you have used the joins you know
- your sentences make sense because you chose the best word.

Find one word to tick and one to improve.

Building on horizontal join to anticlockwise letters Unit 26

1 Trace and write the joins.

wo

oc

og

va

vo

2 Trace and write the words.

wolf

cockerel

frog

van

vole

3 Write the missing word with or without an apostrophe. Finish the punctuation and write the sentences.

The _____ are in the pens by the door_

_____

Most _____ crow loudly_

_____

Is the _____ howl louder than the _____ croak_

_____

4 Tick to show the punctuation you used.

| ? | . | . | ' | ' |

Check:
- you have used the joins you know
- your sentences are properly punctuated.

Find one word to tick and one to improve.

27

Unit 27 G Introducing joins to *s*

1 Trace and write the joins.

as

os

ts

es

us

is

2 Trace and write the words.

was

whose

wants

these

bus

this

3 Choose a word from the box to finish each sentence in the tense shown. Write the sentences.

| were   am   are |

I ___ James' sister. **(present tense)**

We ___ friends but he does annoy me. **(present tense)**

We ___ glad when he was back with us. **(past tense)**

Check:
- you have used the joins you know
- you have written the correct tense.

Find one word to tick and one to improve.

Practising joining *ed* and *ing*   G Unit 28

1 Trace and write the joins.

ed   *ing*

2 Trace and write the words.

liked   *cried*   *smiling*   *licking*

3 Tick and copy sentences which have correct spelling, punctuation and grammar.

Mum maked cakes for tea.

We smiled at our visitors.

The cat was licking its whiskers.

She cried when they left.

They was smiling at us.

Check:
- you have used the joins you know
- you have copied all of the correct sentences.

Find one word to tick and one to improve.

Unit 29 — Assessment

1 Trace and write the words.

can   have   she

does   not   they

has   we   it

could   you

do   he

2 Trace the words and fill the gaps in the table

Pronoun	Full form	Contraction
I	can not	can't
she	could not	
you		haven't
he	does not	
we		don't
they		weren't

3 Write a sentence using pronouns and a contraction.

Capitals Unit 30

1 Trace and write the letters.

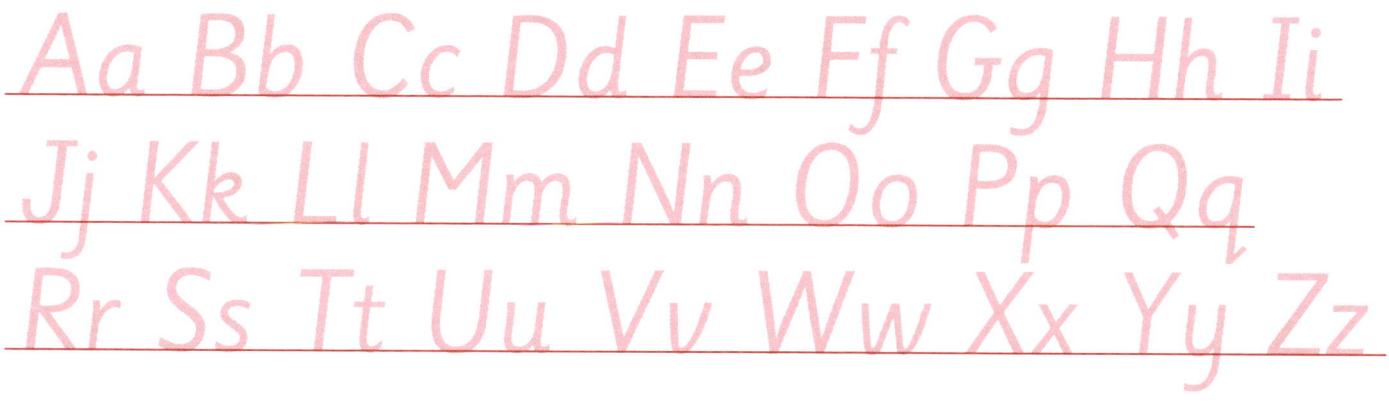

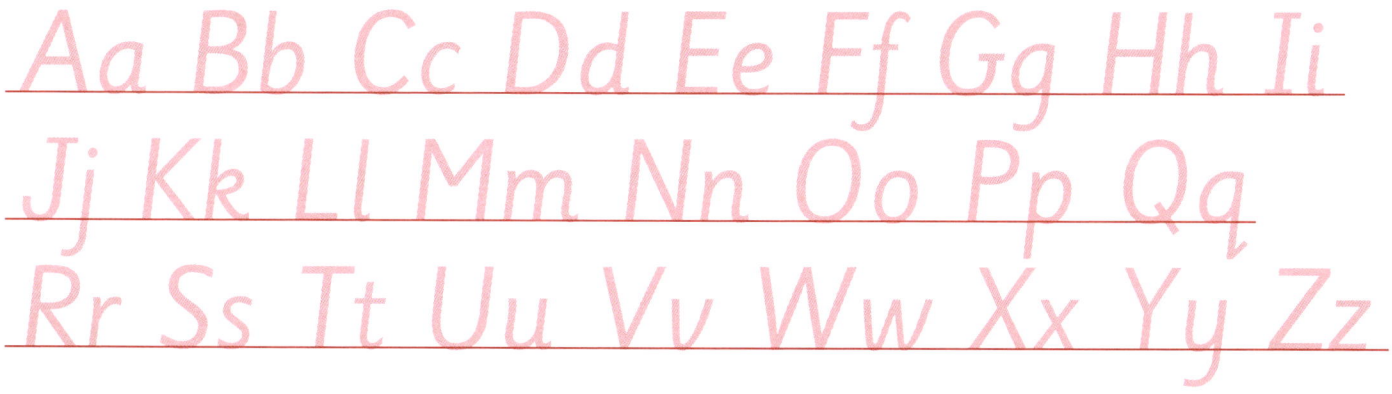

Aa Bb Cc Dd Ee Ff Gg Hh Ii
Jj Kk Ll Mm Nn Oo Pp Qq
Rr Ss Tt Uu Vv Ww Xx Yy Zz

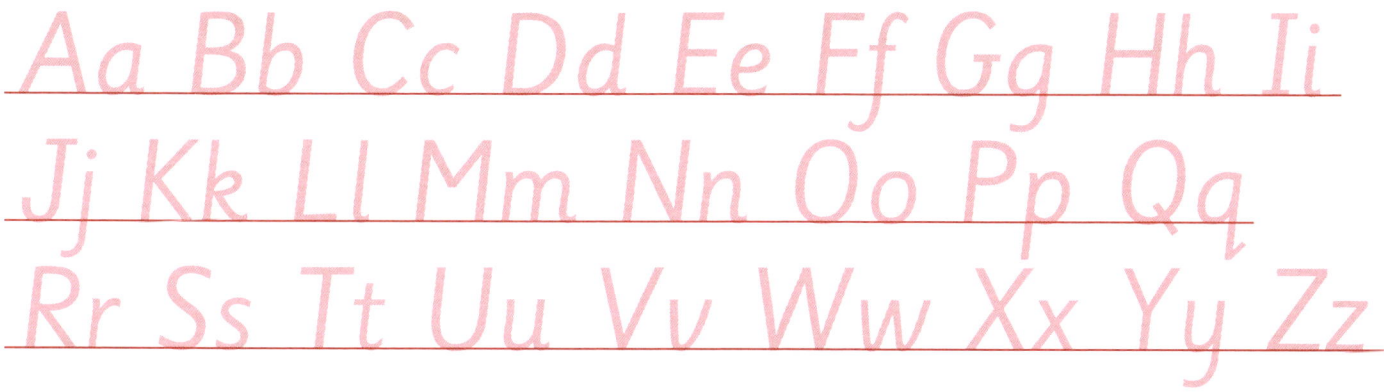

2 Copy the notices.

FIRE EXIT   DANGER   STOP

Check:
- the size of all the letters
- that letters sit on the line unless they have descenders.

Find one word to tick and one to improve.

Certificate

for completing

PENPALS for
Handwriting  2

awarded to

NAME
_____

DATE _____ SIGNED _____

University Printing House, Cambridge CB2 8BS, United Kingdom
One Liberty Plaza, 20th Floor, New York, NY 10006, USA
477 Williamstown Road, Port Melbourne, VIC 3207, Australia
4843/24, 2nd Floor, Ansari Road, Daryaganj, Delhi – 110002, India
79 Anson Road, #06–04/06, Singapore 079906

Cambridge University Press is part of the University of Cambridge.

It furthers the University's mission by disseminating knowledge in the pursuit of education, learning and research at the highest international levels of excellence.

Information on this title: education.cambridge.org

© Cambridge University Press 2015
First published 2015
20 19 18 17 16 15 14

Printed in Poland by Opolgraf

A catalogue record for this publication is available from the British Library

ISBN 978-1-8456-5298-2

Acknowledgements

Illustrations by Marek Jagucki

Cover design and layout by me&him

Authors: Gill Budgell and Kate Ruttle

CAMBRIDGE UNIVERSITY PRESS

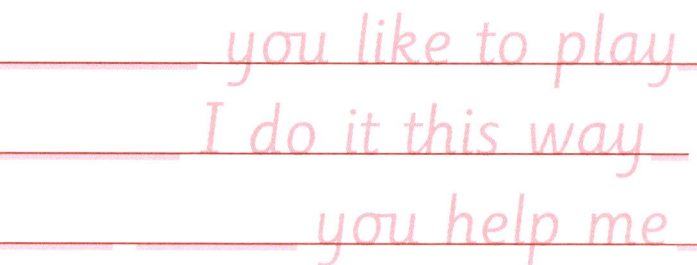

CAMBRIDGE HITACHI

Penpals for Handwriting

Workbook

2

Name _____   Class _____

Penpals *for* Handwriting

Workbook

2

Name .... Class ....

practising diagonal join, no ascender   S Unit 2

1 Trace and write the joins.

ai _____ _____   *ay* _____ _____

2 Trace and write the words.

snail   *train*   *today*

_____   _____   _____

3 Choose *ai* or *ay* to finish the words. Write the words.

pl___ground   r___ny d___   cr___on

_____   _____   _____

4 Write all the days of the week.

_____   _____   _____

_____   _____

_____

Check:
- you have joined *ai* and *ay*
- you have spelled the word correctly.

Find one word to tick and one to improve.

3

PENPALS *for* Handwriting

2

Workbook

Name _____ Class _____